"My total dedication and obsession with photography has taken me on journeys into many remarkable areas throughout Australia. I captured this collection of images using a specialist panoramic camera. Because of the wider field of view, this format enables me to portray the true spirit of Australia on film. Upon viewing these images I am sure you will share with me the tranquility and solitude I experienced whilst capturing the stunning beauty of this country."

PETERLIKIMAGELIBRARY

www.peterlikimages.com

PeterLikPublishing

PO Box 2529 Cairns Queensland 4870 Australia
Telephone: (07) 4053 9000 **Fax:** (07) 4032 1277
sales@peterlik.com.au   **www.peterlik.com.au**

© Peter Lik Publishing   BK06

ISBN 0 95870020 6

Front cover - Uluru - Ayers Rock
Back cover - Fitzroy Island, Queensland
Title page - Lady Musgrave Island, Great Barrier Reef
Intro Page - Three Sisters, Blue Mountains, NSW

A Panoramic Journey Through Australia

Peter Lik

CONTENTS

MAGNIFICENT LANDSCAPES

The diversity of Australia's magnificent landscapes are captured brilliantly by Peter Lik on his Fuji 617 Panoramic Camera. The wide open skylines, vast outback plains and endless deserted beaches all provide magnificent landscapes from which the true essence is captured by Peter's ®Panoscapes. Australia is a land of extremes portrayed by its unique scenery and colourful characters. From the "True Blue", Fair Dinkum Aussie digger, boilin' up his cuppa in a blackened billy in the isolated outback, to the crowded surf beaches of the Gold Coast, and to the exciting bustling city of Sydney metropolis, Australian's have such varied lifestyles, but at the end of the day are all "mates".

The interior of the world's oldest continent provides infinite landscapes which reflect dreamtime magic. The glowing ochre colours of the desert, the snow-covered peaks of the high country, the rolling hills of the Hinterland, and the azure crystal waters of never-ending coastlines, all create the contrasts of colours that Australia is renowned for.

Australia's Great Barrier Reef offers superb diving amongst 1500 species of tropical fish, tropical islands and pristine sand cays.

World Heritage Rainforests are living museums and home to some of the rarest flora and fauna in the world.

Uluru, Ayers Rock is the heart of Australia. Sundown over this awesome monolith reflects the ever-changing hues of the ochre outback. Close by, Kata Tjuta - The Olgas proudly guard the desert floor.

Journey now with Peter through the remotest areas of Australia and discover the incredible beauty of the land downunder.

Mt Kosciusko and the Snowy Mountains.

Wild Flowers of the high country.

In southern parts of Australia, winter transforms the high country into a snow covered wonderland. Mt Kosciusko, Australia's highest mountain at 2228m, and the Snowy Mountains provide excellent skiing on the highest plateau in the Australian continent. The snow clad craggy peaks of Cradle mountain in Tasmania's World Heritage Wilderness reward bushwalkers with spectacular scenery.

Cradle Mountain, Tasmania 7

Kangaroo and Joey

$\mathcal{K}$oalas and Kangaroos are Australia's most lovable marsupials. The young are born tiny and naked, and complete their development in their mothers pouch. Koalas spend most of their lives in the forks of gum trees and sleep up to 19 hours a day. Kangaroos have a tail developed for support, long feet and powerful limbs enabling a swift bounding motion.

The Australian Koala is a marsupial which mothers its young in a pouch.

The true blue Aussie stockman battles the elements of the land and requires only humble abode in which to shelter; often roughly constructed from corrugated iron, timber and anything else that was lying around at the time.

A days mustering would be incomplete without the assistance of the Aussie sheep dog.

Sunflower Field, Toowoomba

$\mathcal{T}$he classic Aussie pub is found almost everywhere in Australia, even in the remotest of towns.

You can always call in and grab a "coldie" with the locals at the watering hole and each of these unique establishments comes complete with its own breed of publican, always ready to spin a good yarn.

The Southern Cross and Comet windmills are traditional Australian monuments which rise majestically from the endless flat open plains. These Australian icons constantly struggle to bring water; the life blood of Australia, to the surface of the dehydrated outback.

Previous Page: Toobrack Station, Queensland

Hebel Hotel

Railway Hotel, Ravenswood

The leaning barn next to the Einasleigh pub portrays the 'she'll be right, mate' attitude of the outback.

Previous Page: Twilight over Sydney Harbour from Lady Macquarie's Chair.

Sydney's Harbour cradles the famous Opera House and Sydney Harbour Bridge. 21

Spectacular Coastlines

The world famous Australian coastline is extremely diverse. The Great Barrier Reef extends 2,300 kms from Cape York to Bundaberg and shelters the North Queensland coast. Cape Tribulation is the only place in the world where two World Heritage areas unite, the Great Barrier Reef and World Heritage Rainforest. Thousands of tropical islands and sand cays display their beauty along this coast. From Tweed Heads to Bega, the New South Wales coastline offers spectacular scenery including the Byron Bay lighthouse, famous surf beaches and fishing villages.

Victoria's Great Ocean Road gives access to some of Australia's most striking coastal scenery, including the magnificent Twelve Apostles and sparkling waters of Wilsons Promontory, Australia's most southerly point. As you continue west to the Eyre Peninsula in South Australia, this corridor offers Australia's most rugged coastline; where towering limestone cliffs drop sheer to the pounding southern ocean. Esperance is a magnificent beach with turquoise waters and pristine white sands.

Along the West Australian coastline the beaches become more protected where you can play with the dolphins at Monkey Mia, relax on the endless Broome beaches, or explore the magnificent Kimberley. The Northern Territory's famous Kakadu National park borders the coast along with the wilderness coastlines of Arnhemland on the Arafura Sea.

Tasmania, the beautiful island boasts the sensational Wineglass Bay, picturesque Coles Bay, and the dramatic views of the Nut, Stanley.

Lady Musgrave Island is surrounded by the perfect coral lagoon. *Previous Page: Hardy's Lagoon, Whitsundays, Queensland.*

$\mathscr{A}$ustralia's Great Barrier Reef is one of the seven natural wonders of the world. This fragile eco-system is home for more than 1,500 species of fish and over 400 different types of coral.

Some 600 continental islands and 350 coral cays are dispersed throughout this natural phenomenon.

The Reef was gazetted a World Heritage area on the 26th October, 1981. The biological and geological complexity of the Reef make it the earth's richest marine habitat.

Whales and dolphins are the most popular mammals of Australian waters.

Reflections of Fraser Island.

Anemone fish add to the enchantment of the Great Barrier Reef

Victoria's landmark, The Twelve Apostles were originally part of the mainland, sculptured by the pounding seas.

Tranquil waters of Merimbula NSW.

$\mathcal{A}$ ustralia's beautiful coastline boasts precipitous cliffs, long wide beaches and idyllic coves. 36,738km of coastline encompasses the largest island on earth. 80% of the 18 million Australian population reap the benefits of living on this magnificent coast.

Twilight over Carnarvon, Western Australia

Opposite Page: Moonrise casts its eerie glow on the Twelve Apostles.

Castaway's Retreat, Welcome Bay, Fitzroy Island.

The pristine sands and turquoise waters of Lake MacKenzie, Fraser Island, Queensland.

A classic North Queensland beach scene at Palm Cove 35

The swirling silica sands of Hill Inlet, Whitsunday Island, Queensland.

The Pinnacles moonscape, Nambung National Park, W.A.

Precipitous sandstone cliffs of the Great Australian Bight, Eucla.

Crystal waters of the Coral Sea

38

WORLD HERITAGE RAINFORESTS

Australian rainforests are our rare and ancient heritage. These living museums are only remnants of the huge forests that once grew throughout Australia. Found here is an astonishing assortment of living fossils, including the largest collection of primitive flowering plants on earth, the most ancient of songbirds and the ancestral lineage of many groups of animals and plants. The wet tropics of North-east Queensland contain the largest continuous areas of rainforest remaining in Australia.

There is only a tiny area of rainforest scattered in patches near the coast, and is much less than 1% of Australia's land mass area. In spite of this small area nearly one half of Australia's bird and plant species are found in the rainforest and well over two-thirds the continents ferns, birds, bat and butterfly species inhabit the rainforest.

The world's rainforests provide us with clean air and water and must be preserved and respected by us all.

Ulysses Butterfly, Queensland

Tchupala Falls, Palmerston National Park, Queensland

Katoomba Falls, Blue Mountains, New South Wales   *Previous Page: Sunrays penetrate the Daintree National Park*

*A*ustralia's rainforests are like windows to the past. They are living museums which are home for beautiful coloured butterflies, croaking frogs, cute possums and many other rare and endangered plant and animal species.

White Lipped Tree Frog

Natural Arch, Springbrook National Park, Queensland

Terrace Falls in the Blue Mountains cascades over thirteen tiers. 45

46 *Cape Tribulation, the only place in the world where two World Heritage areas meet, The Great Barrier Reef and the Rainforest.*

Dorrigo National Park NSW

Sherbrooke Forest, Victoria

Mt Lewis National Park, Queensland

Rugged Outback

Under the southern cross the rugged Australian outback portrays its unique beauty. Uluru - Ayers Rock, the heart of Australia, majestically rises 348m from the desert floor. The rock is 9km in circumference and with the movement of the sun, Uluru displays a magnificent array of fiery red, delicate mauves, blue and pink colours. When rain falls it veils the rock in silver torrents.

Nearby Kata Tjuta, The Olgas reflect dreamtime magic. The tallest dome of Kata Tjuta, Mt Olga is 546 metres above the oasis like Valley of the Winds, that meanders through the rock system.

As the days change, so does the incredible lighting of the outback, providing harsh contrasts or soft colours onto the deserts ridges and gorges of Central Australia. With each day break a new landscape is born.

When this parched environment receives rain from the wet season, the desert is transformed into a region of life. The arteries of the outback river system will flow again and carpets of wildflowers bloom across the terra-firma.

Sleeping in a swag beneath the magical beauty of the southern skies, hearing nothing but the crackle of a burning campfire you can capture the true spirit of the outback.

Moonglow over Chambers Pillar NT

Australia's ancient interior has been sculptured over millions of years by time and nature's elements to create these desert masterpieces. Chambers Pillar and Devil's Marbles are perfect examples of natural monoliths of the rugged outback.

Daybreak over Chamber's Pillar, NT

Previous Page: Spiritual skies over Uluru, NT

Moonlight casts its glow over Devil's Marbles 53

Glowing red domes of Kata Tjuta - The Olgas

Rainbow Valley Reflections

58 *Sundown over Uluru, Australia's heart.*   *Previous Page: Kata Tjuta - The Olgas awakening.*

Magnificent skies of Uluru.

Spinifex bushes, Simpson Desert

Ghost gums reach towards the southern skies 59

Bungle Bungles, Purnululu National Park

The fearsome appearance of the Thorny Devil lizard belies his placid nature.

The glowing red sands of the Simpson Desert.

Overleaf: Twilight reflections over Kakadu National Park, NT.   *The Dreamtime magic of Jessie, a beautiful Aboriginal girl*

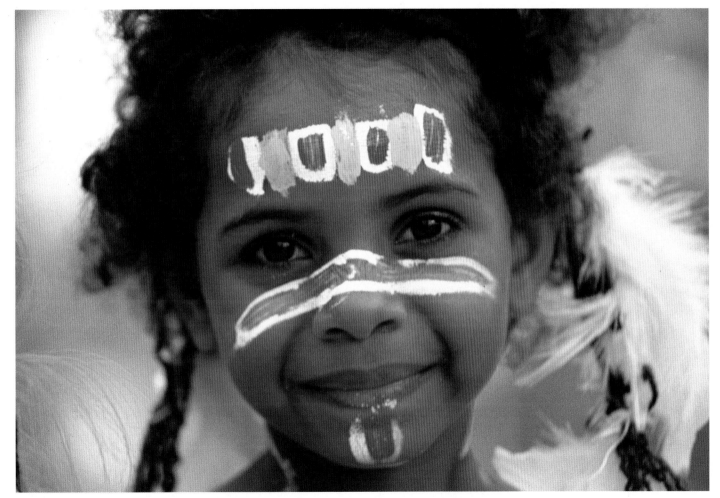

Overleaf: Twilight reflections over Kakadu National Park, NT.   *The Dreamtime magic of Jessie, a beautiful Aboriginal girl*   61

BOOKS BY PETER LIK

- Australia
- Blue Mountains
- Brisbane
- Byron Bay
- Cairns
- Daintree and Cape Tribulation
- Fraser Island
- Gold Coast
- Great Barrier Reef
- Port Douglas
- Sunshine Coast
- Sydney
- The Red Centre
- Townsville and Magnetic Island
- Wildlife
- World Heritage Rainforest

LARGE FORMAT PUBLICATIONS

- "Australia - Images of a Timeless Land"
- San Francisco

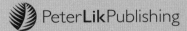